ALSO BY ANDREA BLYTHE

Your Molten Heart / A Seed to Hatch

EVERY GIRL BECOMES THE WOLF

LAURA MADELINE WISEMAN & ANDREA BLYTHE

Every Girl Becomes the Wolf

With Laura Madeline Wiseman

PRAISE FOR TWELVE

"Andrea Blythe's collection of the retold (and often feminist) Brothers Grimm fairy tale, 'The Twelve Dancing Princesses,' is a breath of air at the bottom of the ocean. It's not only fresh, but it's so different and unique that it deserves multiple reads. One of my favorite lines in the book is also something we should all ask ourselves, 'Do you mean it?'"

— JOANNA C. VALENTE, AUTHOR
OF *MARYS OF THE SEA* AND
EDITOR OF *A SHADOW MAP:
WRITING BY SURVIVORS OF
SEXUAL ASSAULT*

"Hearkening back to when Grimm's tales were less fairy, more formidable, Andrea Blythe offers a rhythmic, alliterative retelling of traditional stories that reveal a stark imbalance between genders. An engaging and eerie tribute to the young girls and women who read, dance, and keep things clean, Twelve does exactly what her storyteller suggests of her characters: it 'see[s] the truth beneath the pretty surface.'"

— CHRISTINA M. RAU, ELGIN
AWARD-WINNING AUTHOR OF
LIBERATING THE ASTRONAUTS

"A delightful deviation from the known tale 'The Twelve Dancing Princesses,' Blythe's retelling offers an inspiring and poetic account of what can happen when women take back their power. The language is beautifully selected for each sister's story—and each one has been carefully crafted to have an individual voice, yet we feel the strength of the bond that ties them. Within, we are granted glances into enchantment and passion, to lyrical attractions that will have you spinning breathless from page to page."

— SARA TANTLINGER, BRAM STOKER AWARD-WINNING AUTHOR OF *THE DEVIL'S DREAMLAND*

"The prose poems of *Twelve* shimmer like precious stones, each reflecting the original fairy tale in strange, beautiful, and unsettling ways—and when set together, they become a mosaic of womanhood in all its forms."

— CASSANDRA ROSE CLARKE, RHYSLING AWARD-WINNING AUTHOR OF *SACRED SUMMER*

TWELVE

This is a work of fiction. All of the characters, organizations, and events portrayed are either products of the author's imagination or used fictitiously.

TWELVE: POEMS INSPIRED BY THE BROTHERS GRIMM FAIRY TALE

Text Copyright © 2020 by Andrea Blythe.

All rights reserved.

No part of this book may be reproduced in any form or by any electronic or mechanical means, including information storage and retrieval systems, without written permission from the author and publisher, except for the use of brief quotations in a book review.

Cover illustration by Yana Germann.

Edited by Holly Lyn Walrath.

Published by Interstellar Flight Press, Houston, Texas.

www.interstellarflightpress.com

ISBN (eBook): 978-1-7338862-4-6

ISBN (Paperback): 978-1-7338862-3-9

ISBN (Hardback): 978-1-7338862-5-3

First Edition: 2020

TWELVE

POEMS INSPIRED BY THE BROTHERS GRIMM FAIRY TALE

ANDREA BLYTHE

INTERSTELLAR FLIGHT PRESS

CONTENTS

Prelude: The Shoes	1
The First Sister	5
The Second Sister	7
The Third Sister	9
The Fourth Sister	13
The Fifth Sister	17
The Sixth Sister	19
The Seventh Sister	21
The Eighth and Ninth Sisters	23
The Tenth Sister	25
The Eleventh Sister	27
The Twelfth Sister	31
Author's Note	35
Acknowledgments	43
About the Author	45
About the Cover Artist	47
Interstellar Flight Press	49
Recent Releases from Interstellar Flight Press	51

PRELUDE: THE SHOES

It began with the shoes and the expense they entailed. Twelve pairs piled in tatters—soles worn through, satin frayed. Shoes ruined during the course of each night and replaced each day.

The King's daughters would not explain the shoes—what had occurred in the dark hours of the night for them to be used so harshly. They had secrets, selves they kept hidden. Intolerable. He could not abide such disobedient silence. Daughters were meant to be placid, pure, and idle beauties who accepted their role as tokens in the bartering of treaties. They were not meant to have minds of their own.

> (*The king, we note, did not ask the queen or his own aging mother about the kinds of secrets girls kept. It did not occur to him and, as he did not ask, they each held their peace.*)

He sought the aid of wise and brave men—scholars, doctors, princes, and priests. He issued a proclamation: whomsoever discovered the truth of the shoes would win the daughter of his choosing. But as princesses are no cheap prize, the suitors would only be granted three nights to answer the mystery or meet the ax.

Men journeyed to the palace in droves. Sent to watch over the princesses, they stood to the test, failed, and died. The king watched their heads tumble into the dirt and despaired of ever learning the secrets of his daughters.

Then came a soldier, wounded and returned home from battle. A common man, rough-hewn, scarred, not as young as he used to be. The king held no hope, sent the soldier to face his three nights, and readied the executioner.

Upon his return, the soldier related a wondrous tale of stairways under floorboards, fantastical gardens ripe with glittering silver, gold, and diamond fruit, magical boats to enchanted islands, and fairy princes who danced with the princesses all night long—until their shoes shredded under the strain of holding them aloft.

TWELVE

(The soldier, we note, did not credit the old woman on the road, who had ensured this success by warning him to avoid the drugged wine and gifting him a cloak of invisibility.)

The twelve princesses were called before the King and evidence of their indiscretions was presented. When they realized their secret had been flayed open before the court and falsehood would not spare them, they each hid away their feelings of rage, sorrow, relief, fear, indignation, or shame and did the only thing they could —they confessed and begged forgiveness.

The king, grinning with his victory, asked the soldier which princess he desired for a wife. The soldier chose the eldest—and the king was doubly pleased. The girl was nearly a spinster anyway, and he still had so many other young daughters to trade away for kingdoms and power.

The king was at his ease. The underground realms would be sealed. His daughters returned to their rooms under watchful eyes. All was set right again. He had reclaimed the order he commanded, and there would be no more secrets.

THE FIRST SISTER

The white of her wedding dress evoked not innocence but the heat of her rage. Her husband—old soldier, trickster, liar—sweated under her incandescence. His hands blistered as he took her arm and steered her in procession down the aisle.

He chose her because she was the eldest. Because the weight of history was braided in her brown hair and piled on her head, just as his sins were written in the scars mapping his body.

As the soldier and his prize stared at each other across the marriage bed, he felt distant battlefields in his bones. *I won't take anything you are not ready to give,* he said, keeping his distance, patient.

Her blood spit within her veins like dragon fire. In reply, she ravaged him, raking his bare skin with clawed fingers, biting until she drew blood, taking every ounce of pleasure from him—as she had once taken from the dancing.

She dreamed herself poisonous and woke in the morning to fresh resolution. Gathering herbals from a sister's garden, she brewed belladonna tea, steeped mushrooms in aconite, and baked hemlock-seasoned lark into a meat pie.

Her husband thanked her for her generosity and tipped his teacup into a vase of dahlias, declared an aversion to mushrooms, and declined the pie, his stomach overfull for anything so rich.

She tossed foxglove leaves into salads, cooked creamy mandrake au gratin, and slipped cyanide into his wine.

The soldier picked his way through the greens. Knocked the au gratin clumsily to the floor. Raised his goblet high to his wife's health, drank deep, and did not die, having already switched one cup for another.

They played a game of poisoning, death always at the edges of every smile, every kiss and touch and caress.

One of these days you're going to succeed in poisoning me, he said, voice graveled as he rasped his bristled chin against the softness of her throat and scoured her bare hip bones with war-weathered hands. *And then, won't you just regret.*

Such, she said between gasps of breath. *Such regret.*

THE SECOND SISTER

She would not give up the dancing—not even for her sister's wedding, spinning past young lords who failed to keep pace, past the musicians who played until their fingers ached and cramped and could play no more, past the exhausted, departing guests, past the servants clearing away evidence of the celebration, the clatter of platters and utensils marking a beat for her every skipping step—dancing well past the dawn and into the day, her family later finding her in a field, the tattered remains of her shoes marking the path, her body given up to exhaustion, hair limp and tangled in the dewy clovers, shivering in her sweat-damp dress—even in sleep her muscles twitching out their desire for the allemande or cinque-pace or minuet—and when she woke, she resumed her dance, pirouetting through the halls, the library, the sitting rooms—unable to explain her need—twirling, twirling, twirling—an unstoppable dizzy whirl, even when her shoes gave out, leather soles shredding, stockings tearing, leaving her to pirouette on the bare pads of her feet, dancing even as her feet became raw and began to bleed, the red of it wrapping around her toes like crimson shoes—but it didn't matter how she tore and bled for no one could touch her—the dancing carried her beyond the weight of obligations, beyond the pain of the dirt and stones grinding into her soles—every step lifting her higher, up past treetops and mountains, past clouds and birds in flight—drifting like a kite on the breeze.

THE THIRD SISTER

The library beckoned, and she answered the call, slipping herself in between the welcoming shelves, letting the stillness and quiet seep into her, the soft motes of dust alighting on her skin, and the smell of the leather-bound volumes soothing the aches of her body and spirit.

The books whispered their longing to be read. She plucked them from the shelves at random, gathering them up and cradling them in her arms. She laid them out upon a table and savored the creak of their spines as they opened.

She read—words unveiling worlds more astounding than the glittering gold and silver gardens she and her sisters found hidden under their floorboards. She read until the candles burned low, until her eyes felt like sand and her vision blurred, until her spine bent into a bow, and she fell into a restful sleep, a treatise on the alchymical uses of plants as a pillow.

As time passed, she faded into the library more and more—so many hours at a stretch, the days and nights blurred together in a litany of poetry and candlelight. She read and she wrote, the nib of her plume scratching out the results of her research, ink-splotched pages filled so thickly with text they appeared black. When visiting students and scholars spoke with her, she held discourse on the natural world and the worlds beyond, leaving them wide-eyed and awed when they returned to their universities.

Her father sent messengers to draw her back into the sitting rooms and gardens and ballrooms, the light and airy places where princesses belonged. When this failed, he stormed into the library himself, prepared to drive her out with the thunder of his speech and the lightning of his hand. The tall stone shelves greeted him with their towering height—full of tomes of natural history and philosophy and mathematics alongside the ramblings of novelists and the fancies of poets—all the crushing weight of knowledge pressing down upon him. He searched and found only books and silence, the whisper of his own breath loud in his ears. Eventually, the eerie quiet unsettled and drove him back to the clattering noise of the court, to the voices and laughter and music that filled up his thoughts and hours.

The library became her realm. She slept on the nests of old discarded pamphlets and nourished herself on the pages she consumed. Over time, her skin paled and hair thinned. Her hands became marked with paper cuts, nails black with ink. She padded through the shelves like a specter, leaving a wake of near-completed tracts and treatises and historical accounts at her feet—

TWELVE

treasures scholars discovered and smuggled out into the world, published anonymously to great acclaim and outrage. She was rarely seen, more mythic creature than person—a ghost some said, a monster, a patron saint of the stacks. It was a blessing, it was said, or a curse, claimed others, to see her and have her look upon you. She might read you and find in your flesh the story that shapes you.

THE FOURTH SISTER

The dead were all around her—princes, scholars, dukes, soldiers, blacksmiths, heralds, butlers, chancellors—all the ghosts of the men who believed a princess was a trophy, men who thought themselves more cunning than her sisters, men who thought they could solve a simple mystery of tattered shoes, men who inevitably failed and were rewarded for their failure with the executioner's axe. She had hated them when they were alive, hated the way they stood watching her, watching her sisters, the way their grins filled their faces as they sized up each princess, from woman to girl, deciding before the game ended which one they would choose. She had told herself it didn't matter when their heads fell from their shoulders—the men made a choice, after all, to come to the palace and set themselves against the wits of princesses.

She told herself she was not responsible, even though she watched her sister drug each man into a slumber, each man snoring away while twelve princesses slipped down into the shadow realms where fairy princes fitted their graceful hands to the waist of each princess and pulled them into a spinning intoxication of movement and laughter. In the shiny glow of the dancing, she let herself forget how the blood of all those men soaked into the deep, black earth, seeping past roots and worms to drip upon their heads. She was not surprised to discover the smear of that guilt followed her up into the light, where the dead men lingered in the corners of the castle halls—silhouette figures flickering in the inconsistent candlelight. The dead men gathered in mirrored surfaces, clustered in dark alcoves, flared in the flickering of fireplaces—each indistinct from the next, the many becoming one in their identical deaths. Their faces had no eyes, only empty black sockets, but they watched her just the same. No throats or tongues or teeth either, but their voices stalked her with accusations, a sound like distant echoes or a whistling in the eaves. We just wanted a piece of beauty, just a kiss, just a screw, just you or a sister, not too much to ask, no, not too much. They hovered over her and kept her from sleep. They brushed against her, spiderweb soft, and denied her any ease.

She told them to leave her be, but they did not listen. She lit candles before saints and knelt at altars, palms pressed together, knees wracked with pain. Let them be banished, dispersed, released from the burden of haunting, she prayed, so she might be released from them. She sought the aid of witches, begging for spells to banish the dead, to sweep them from the palace rooms like dust and prevent them from ever returning. When these methods did not free her, she tried to escape—urged her father to marry her off to a distant lord, someone to carry her away from the dead and their why, why, whys echoing in her head. She let a living man claim her to escape the dead ones and traveled far, far away to a stranger's home—only to find the dead men followed her. They would never leave, always hungry, always needy, pale palms reaching out to claim her, wispy tendrils of fingers stroking her skin. Despair settled upon her like a shroud.

It might have enveloped her completely, if the heaviness had not reminded her of the thick quilts her grandmother spent hours embroidering. One could stitch all their sorrows into cloth, her grandmother believed, all that hardship and anxiety could be mended through needle and thread, transformed from a cold weight into a warm comfort. She did not have her grandmother's skill, clumsy fingers continually pricked by the needle—but maybe she could hook each spirit with a sharp point, gather them together, and stitch them into something more manageable, a blanket or drape or cowl. It would take years to collect and contain all the dead, but if they were to be her burden, then maybe they could be the kind of burden she could fold up and pack away.

THE FIFTH SISTER

When she was young, she ate apples whole, swallowing the core and bitter seeds along with the white flesh. Her sisters joked that a tree would take root and grow inside her. Now, as her belly swelled, her sisters whispered behind their hands, not quite meeting her eyes. Her father said, *Sin*; the nurse said, *Such a shame, poor thing*; the nurse said, *It will be alright, poppet*. They all let her be tucked away into a small corner of the castle where the roundness of her belly could not be seen. *Baby*, she thought, prodding her stomach—but maybe it was the apple seed after all, growing, roots curling down, green tendrils stretching for light. Maybe the tree would branch out through her insides and burst from her skin. Maybe it would grow her right into the ground like a dryad, her limbs becoming branches, skin thick with bark, head crowned in bright, swaying leaves.

Or maybe it was some other creature entirely—wolf, basilisk, hound, cockatrice—something furred, scaled, clawed. There was no way to tell, and this both terrified and fascinated her. She knew the court spoke in hushed tones of the lasciviousness of fairies, of what indecencies other than dancing may have transpired in the dark realm. But her fairy prince had not touched her, save to steer her across the ballroom floor. Maybe she had merely swallowed a mote of dust from that dark world, seed enough to take root inside her. Or maybe a spark of light reflecting off one of the golden gardens inspired the idea of life within her belly. Any small fraction of magic could have settled itself under her skin.

Every time the creature moved, she sighed—imagined branch or paw or infant palm, imagined all the things she could carry. A part of her wanted to pull back her own skin, peer inside, and learn what grew. Another part enjoyed the anticipation.

THE SIXTH SISTER

She vanished and was forgotten. Only her room stood in remembrance:

The deflated silk form of her nightgown—emptied of its owner—nestled beneath rumpled covers. One crumpled sleeve resting on a pillow still depressed with the shape of her head.

The small poetry book rested open, a drop of candle wax marring its yellowed page.

The glass of water settled half-empty on the nightstand, an impression of lips on the rim.

Dolls stood observant on the shelf, keeping their silence.

Dust motes floated in suspension. Undrifting.

Daisies failed to wither. The vase of water never lost its crystalline transparency, never bloomed green algae.

Smoke remained a stagnant coiled plume above the blackened candlewick.

The room never changed. Spiders never thickened the corners with cobwebs. Mice never nested in the discarded fabric and fluff of the ottoman. Nothing ever rotted or decayed.

A moment held captive.

Not even the light shifted from its quiet noctilucence.

THE SEVENTH SISTER

All things broken down to their constituent parts reveal truth.

Her rooms reflected this belief with their cacophony of flasks and vials and jars full of sulphurs and lye and mercury, mortar and pestles stained with the crushed remains of seed and leaf and mineral, various alembics and retorts distilling foul-smelling liquids over small flames. The tables scattered with charts and papers filled with notes and formulae. A portion of the palace gardens reserved for her personal cultivation of plants with a multitude of uses.

She could determine the exact chymical content of a mineral compound or distill the essence of flowers—the milky sap of a poppy rendered down into a sleeping draught or concentrated further into poison. Even lead could be transmuted into gold, if you understood the intricacies of the material world.

But she had a greater mystery to unlock—the alchymy of the soul.

She began with the body, examining creatures of lesser form, creatures trapped in formaldehyde—mice, snakes, birds, cats, lizards, rabbits. She dismantled them into their base elements—hair, skin, scale, teeth, muscle, bone—pieces labeled and categorized for further study.

As she grew closer to her understanding of the factors that bound the sulphuric soul to mercurial flesh, she needed to move her research closer to her true goal—the study of man.

A human being had to be unmade in order to be made, the salt-and-water body opened and picked apart in order to reveal its secrets. But it was infinitely more difficult to find specimens for such a project without misunderstanding and censure. One could not perform such work on the great lords and ladies of the household, and the servants quickly learned to fear her, shying away whenever she approached. Corpses wrapped in shrouds, on the other hand, were too far detached from the soul that once animated them.

So she turned to the only specimen remaining. She laid herself before the crucible, prepared to render down and clarify her own body and soul into their purest form.

THE EIGHTH AND NINTH SISTERS

By the time the household discovered the hoard hidden away in the twins' chambers—the silver candlesticks, gold brocade, casks of wine, strands of pearls, individual earrings, porcelain dolls, embroidered pillows, broken lockets, brass keys, crystal vases, books of psalms, tin soldiers, cracked looking glasses, and purses filled with coins, autumn leaves, and stones—all stuffed under beds, piled behind the curtains, and overflowing the cabinets like a dragon's hoard—the twins themselves had already absconded, the brown locks of their shorn hair discarded upon their trove as though this, too, was treasure.

It was said a countess was robbed upon the road to the castle—one hand plucking the jeweled pendant from her neck, the other slitting her throat—both laughing as the blood adorned the fine dress of the countess like rubies.

Thus, the Black Fox was born—myth, legend, murderer, hero. It was said the Black Fox was a master thief. No, no, it was said the Black Fox was an entire company of bandits. The Black Fox could steal anything—jewels hidden inside castle keeps, entire towers full of gold or the tower itself, kisses and secrets and lives. The Black Fox could become invisible, could travel leagues with a single step. The Black Fox was hypnotically handsome and could seduce amiable ladies and young lords alike. The Black Fox kept such a trove of stolen treasure, he could buy an entire kingdom. The Black Fox was a savior of the poor and the meek. The Black Fox was a devil, a trickster god. The Black Fox was just a clever man of flesh and blood. The Black Fox was the child of Death itself.

No one ever said the Black Fox was a pair of twin sisters bearing shorn hair, leather breeches, and a set of short swords. No one ever said two girls could carve open the world like an oyster, taking all its pearls and swallowing the meat. No one ever believed two girls could take and take and take—for no other reason than they knew they could.

> *(But their sisters knew. They felt the self-same hunger within their bones, and so they said nothing.)*

The Black Fox, in the end, was immortal, stories of his ongoing adventures never dying. Decades later—long after one sister died from a stabbing in a drunken brawl and the other was hanged in a town square—people still clustered in the dim corners of inns, whispered the name and shuddered.

THE TENTH SISTER

Princesses were not made for kitchens, but the yeasty, warm scent of bread baking drew her down into the heat, where the head cook huffed at her presence, irritated, and would not let her touch the spoons or bowls or cupboards or rollers, ushering her to the side where her silk skirts would gather no stains and her hands would remain clean and soft. She stood in her corner and watched the cooks work, floured hands kneading dough, forming rolls and baguettes, shaping sweet meat pies and cookies and cakes. The assemblage of cooks laughed and sang as they worked. They gossiped when they forgot the princess was there. One young cook in particular—about her own age—had a belly-deep laugh that made the princess smile. The cook was not as neat as the others, tucking loose strands of hair behind her ear with jam-sticky fingers, wiping her sweaty brow with the back of her wrist and trailing a line of flour across her forehead. Sometimes the young cook would bring the princess treats fresh from the oven, a still-hot macaroon or steaming slice of pie that burned the roof of the princess' mouth, but she accepted the scalding in exchange for the honey of the girl's smile. *How do you do it?* the princess asked. *Let me show you,* answered the cook and tugged her down to the tables and cutting boards, to the stoves and ovens. The cook guided the hands of the princess, leading them in the sifting of flour, cracking of eggs, mixing of ingredients, and filling of molds. She taught her all the recipes she knew by heart and showed her the rest kept in the large book she revered. They consumed one another in whispers and glances, dough-gummy fingers twisting together, arms grazing as they passed between counters and ovens. At night, they untangled the laces of their skirts, uncaged themselves of corsets, peeling each other open like rare fruit. They licked the sweetness from each other's flesh, a secret joy discovered on the tips of their tongues. Princesses were not made for kitchens or cooks, but it didn't matter. They spent days in the heat of the kitchen and nights in the heat of each other. Their love tasted like salt and sugar, like sweet pastry and bread pudding. It wouldn't last. Nothing ever did. Pastries grew hard, bread bloomed mold. You savored it while it was fresh, or it would grow stale.

THE ELEVENTH SISTER

If she learned nothing else from her sisters, it was this: women kept each other's secrets. A secret was a fragile, dangerous thing. It was something you guarded deep within the cage of your heart, something you never dared let escape. Cross your heart, hope to die.

And yet, it had been a woman who betrayed them—a woman who met the soldier upon the road one day and gave him the means to discover the truth, who stopped the tide of tattered shoes.

It was never about the dancing, which left her indifferent. The dancing was merely a tether that bound her and her sisters together in secrecy, a bond strong as enchantment, a sweetness tasted amongst themselves and no other. To speak the truth of it aloud would be a violation, a rending, and yet it was spoken— the cord severed, her sisters spiraling loose and lost to their own worlds of private adventures, exploits they did not deign to share with her.

She did not blame the soldier for this fracturing. Every man she ever knew claimed rights to the women around him, to their blood and bone and soul.

All her animosity she reserved for the old woman, and she resolved to find her, to demand retribution or explanation. Hope to die, stick a needle in your eye.

She packed a sack and journeyed west. It was, so far as she knew, the direction from which the soldier had come and the way most likely to lead to the old woman.

At the first crossroads, she stopped and considered. *Which way did the old woman go?* she asked of no one in particular.

The wind howled, pushing her back in the direction she had come. The dust kicked up, stung her eyes, and scratched the back of her throat. The trees whispered amongst themselves, ignoring her in their idle gossip.

You're of no help, she replied and plucked a hair from her head. She let the strand fall and drift and curl into the dirt, the spiral of it pointing her further west.

When she reached the next crossroads, she stopped again. *Which way did the old woman go?* she asked.

The sun glared down, scalding her neck. The stones caught her feet and tripped her up. A nearby stream babbled nonsense.

She sighed and plucked another hair from her head.

She continued on in this way, pausing at each crossing, asking her question, and always met with the world's indifference or animosity. Each time she plucked a hair, each time she took its counsel.

One day, she stood at a crossroads and asked, as she always did, *Which way did the old woman go?*

In reply, a puddle offered its silvered surface for reflection. She saw herself—wire white hair, wrinkled face, bowed spine. She was weathered and tired. Her hands were gnarled and her hips ached.

So this is where you've gone, she told the old woman in the puddle. *I've been looking and looking.*

Looking and looking, mimicked the old woman.

Why did you do it? she asked.

The old woman answered, *Why?*

She considered the question. *I don't know. I only know this: I would have kept your secrets, kept them safe and close and never told them. Cross my heart, hope to die.*

Stick a needle in your eye, the old woman repeated in time with her.

Do you mean it?

Mean it, the old woman confirmed.

She smiled, relieved, and settled her creaking body onto the ground. She leaned close to the old woman, who drew close to her, and they began to whisper amongst themselves all they knew.

THE TWELFTH SISTER

Dim light filtered through the boarded-up windows of the room where her sisters and she once slept in a tidy row. It had been so long. Dust settled into the carvings of the headboards and cobwebs drooped in the corners of the room. She once believed the magic of the dancing would last forever, but now—even as she stared down into the dark staircase beneath the floorboards—it seemed a dream.

When her father sealed up the doorway with a thick iron encasement, she had wept tears heavy with the loss. It took years of stepping within every hollow tree and mushroom ring to find her way back. In the end, it was water, time, and rust that did the trick. The iron nails securing the encasement eventually became brittle, breaking away under a few stout blows of her hammer.

If she felt any sense of hesitation, she did not show it. She had prepared for this return—wearing sturdy traveling boots and breeches instead of flimsy dancing shoes and silk. She bore two satchels, carrying all the accoutrement for a long journey.

She stepped down into the cool twilight glow of the underground, pressing her hand against the wall to maintain her balance on the mossy stairs. When she reached the path, the air was winter-cold, cutting through her jacket deep into her bones. The gravel path crunched beneath her boots as she passed the overgrown avenues, the orchards with their glittering trees fading. The silver and gold leaves were tarnished and crumbling into metallic powder. The diamond fruit rotted into dull stone on the ground, little granite worms crawling in and out of the cores.

The small boats at the lake were leached of all magic. They knocked against each other—a soft, hollow, mournful sound that made her heart ache. They could not stay afloat, their hulls leaking. Many were swamped and half sunk—one so consumed it sat on the lakebed, the water inside oily and viscous. She climbed into one that seemed to have will enough to hold her and rowed herself out onto the lake, the split wood of the oars cutting into her palms.

The island, too, had weathered and aged in the time she'd been away, the docks sagging, the pathways overgrown with amber weeds. The pavilion where they had whirled through the night with their charming fairy princes smelled of decay, the tiles cracked and mildewed. She picked up an overturned chair and sat, letting a wistfulness come over her as if she was the fallen queen of a sad, dead world.

At the whisper of shuffling feet, she reached for the

TWELVE

knife at her belt. A bent half-starved creature stood at the periphery. The joyless thing bore ragged grey hair and threadbare clothing. The face was wrong—the mouth too large, the cheeks too sharply angled, the eyes black and hard. It was a monstrous, fairy face. But she recognized him for her once handsome prince.

She smiled, and he held out his hand to her. In the distance, the slow pulse of music tinkled, trying to wake itself up after such long silence. Her muscles twitched, responding to the spell's song. He wanted to woo her again, the building of magic granting him the glittering veneer of beauty.

She collapsed her smile. *I didn't come for you*, she said. And *I don't want to dance.*

The glamour fell and the fairy hunched over as if aged by the effort. These creatures had needed them, she realized. They had drawn from the princesses some power—youth, beauty, innocence, vigor. It didn't matter what. When the dancing ended and the door sealed, that sustenance went with it and it had all gone wrong. Or, maybe it had always been wrong and it was only illusion that kept her sisters and her from seeing the truth beneath the pretty surface.

She stood and the fairy's eyes gleamed. He reached out again and the music swelled, magic flooding the pavilion and wrapping itself around her like a cord. When she was a child, she would have gladly taken his gnarled hand, stepping into the twirling flow of the dancing for a night's worth of something wondrous.

But she was no longer a child.

She pulled away from the power that tried to control her and made her way back down to the docks, ignoring the creature's plaintive calls. The underground was immense, brimming with beautiful, dangerous, alluring realms—all waiting for some industrious adventurer, some brave figure like her to discover them.

AUTHOR'S NOTE

I've often struggled against the idea that there was one kind of story for me—grow up, get married, have kids, and live happily ever after. When I played dolls as a girl, I rarely played house. My Barbie had Things To Do. She owned her own home, had a career to strive for, and the world to travel. If she had a young one to care for, they were often adopted—the presence of a man or partner unnecessary.

One might think a love for fairy tales would be contrary to such leanings, considering how many stories end with the heroine being rescued by and then married to a prince. I've certainly recognized over the years the problematic nature of many fairy tales. The women and girls in these stories often fall into two categories: good (pure-hearted, sweet-natured, and beautiful) or evil (spoiled, wicked, demanding, and ugly). They also don't seem to have much agency of their own, falling under spells that leave them helpless until rescue arrives. Such criticisms are fair and worth talking about.

AUTHOR'S NOTE

Yet, my interest and love for fairy tales is unwavering.

One of the things that draws me to these stories is that they are often centered around women, offering a heroine's journey distinct from Joseph Campbell's hero's journey in *The Hero With a Thousand Faces*. Theodora Goss presents this concept on her blog, describing a number of steps in the journey, such as leaving home, traveling through a dark forest, finding friends or helpers, being tested, and finding a true home (to name a few).[1]

It's the journey (not the ending) that always fascinated me the most—the heroine facing the dangers of the dark forest on her own, using her own cleverness to outwit a witch, or showing kindness to a creature (that may later come to her aid). Not every battle requires the clash of swords or the slaying of a dragon to win. Sometimes it's a matter of sorting lentils from the ashes.

"The Twelve Dancing Princesses" is one of my favorite tales. It begins as a strangely compelling mystery, with the king and all his court wondering what could possibly be happening each night for his twelve daughters to be dancing their shoes to pieces. As the tale goes on, it's revealed that the princesses spend their nights traveling to an underground realm—lush and sparkling with orchards of silver, gold, and diamond—where they dance the night away with handsome princes. When one night a soldier follows the princesses using an invisibility cloak and reveals the truth, he is rewarded with his choice of bride.

AUTHOR'S NOTE

Although, like many fairy tales, "The Twelve Dancing Princesses" ends in marriage, it is different in that no one comes off as being particularly *nice*, let alone good or pure. This is especially true in the Brothers Grimm version of the story. The king locks his daughters in their room each night and chops off the heads of all the suitors who fail to figure out what his daughters are up to. The princesses blithely drug the men into a stupor—thus condemning them to death—just so they can wander off for a night of dancing. The soldier who discovers their secret tricks them in turn and stalks them through the underground realm. Even the suitors losing their heads don't dredge up much sympathy, as they knowingly risk death because they think women are simple enough trophies to be won.

No one is a clear hero or villain.

Trapped by their situation and locked into their rooms each night like treasure to be hoarded, the twelve princesses devise a means of escape.[2] Each night they disappear into another world, where they dance to their heart's content. Dancing may seem like a frivolous desire, but when one's world is so tightly constrained, any means of claiming space can seem immeasurable. It's understandable that—in the face of having that escape and freedom taken away—these women might devise a plan to drug the suitors each night, even if it means their death.

There is power in the fact that they enjoyed pleasure for pleasure's sake and never apologized.

AUTHOR'S NOTE

I would like to claim that what drew me to write about "The Twelve Dancing Princesses" was its feminist slant. But the truth is that it was really a question of mathematics.

Since it had etched itself into my consciousness since I was a kid, I assumed I knew the Brothers Grimm story by heart. Upon rereading the tale as an adult, however, I was surprised to discover that, after all is done, the soldier selects the eldest daughter for his bride—not the youngest as I had always believed.

Most fairy tales have multiple variations, and "The Twelve Dancing Princesses" is no exception. Therefore, I must have read another version of the story —a version that apparently I could not find. Resources such as Sur La Lune[3] pointed me to versions in which the number of princesses, the form of enchantment (if any), and the type of hero all changed—but none were the version I remembered. Maybe it had never existed.[4]

Well, okay, that's fine, I thought. After all, it would be kind of gross for a grown man to be choosing the youngest daughter, who would have been what? Fifteen? How old would she have been anyway?

I started to work out the math. Assuming that these were fairly young women, as most fairy tales present them to be, then if the eldest was twenty-five and the queen gave birth to a daughter once a year for twelve years, then the youngest would be around thirteen—far too young to be getting married. More likely, there would have been gap years in which there were no babies, so the ages could have ranged as widely as the youngest being ten and the eldest being thirty or more.

AUTHOR'S NOTE

However, if twins or triplets were involved, that would compress the timeline and complicate it even further, so . . .

Nevermind. The eldest was chosen to wed the soldier. Considering who she was in the story—a woman who instigated the drugging of the men, led her sisters down into a strange world, and teased her youngest sister for being scared—would she be happy about her situation? Would she quietly accept marriage to a stranger who took away her nights of dancing?

I don't think so. I think she'd be furious.

When the soldier arrives to discover the secret of the tattered shoes, the youngest princess has a sense of foreboding. "I feel very strange," she says. "Some misfortune is certainly about to befall us."

The misfortune that comes is this: The truth is revealed and the dancing is put to an end, delivering the twelve princesses back to the ordinary world—a return to the obligations of the court and the expectations of society. The king would expect them to fall into the proper behavior, to be kind and quiet and complacent. In other words, to be good, marriageable girls.

The king would be a fool.

Women who are clever enough to outsmart dozens of suitors in the pursuit of nightly dancing would not go gently back to their sitting rooms to quietly embroider pillows or paint tables. They would fight back with poisons or alchemy, find solitude and silence in books, and accept the comfort of honey-sweet smiles. They would rove and vanish and tear through the world. They would claw their way back to magic and beauty and power.

They might even choose marriage or motherhood. Both are their own adventures, requiring measures of strength and wisdom.

The trap is when one ending is presented as the only true and meaningful ending. The heroine's journey is vast with possibilities, the roads fork and then fork again. The power comes in the choosing.

Notes

1. "The Heroine's Journey," Theodora Goss, October 2014, https://theodoragoss.com/2014/10/17/the-heroines-journey.

2. Some versions of the tale have the women under an enchantment. However, in the Grimm version, there is no mention of spells or the need to break them, which implies that the young women are acting under their own agency—which is part of the feminist reading of the tale. Mari Ness presents an excellent discussion of this in her essay, "Enchantment, Death, and Footwear: The Twelve Dancing Princesses," published at Tor.com.

3. Surlalunefairytales.com.

4. Turns out it did exist, but not as I remembered. While researching for this author's note, I rediscovered

AUTHOR'S NOTE

the children's book edition of "The Twelve Dancing Princesses," retold by Marianna Mayer and beautifully illustrated by Kinuko Y. Craft. I remember reading and rereading this book, sometimes just to admire the illustrations featuring stunning princesses in luxurious dresses, vibrant fantastical ballrooms, and glittering avenues of trees made of silver, gold, and diamond.

ACKNOWLEDGMENTS

"The Tenth Sister" was first published in *Write Like You're Alive*, Zoetic Press, 2016.

ABOUT THE AUTHOR

Andrea Blythe bides her time waiting for the apocalypse by writing speculative poetry and fiction. She is the author of *Your Molten Heart / A Seed to Hatch* (2018) a collection of erasure poems created from the pages of Trader Joe's Fearless Flyers, and coauthor of *Every Girl Becomes the Wolf* (Finishing Line Press, 2018), a collaborative chapbook written with Laura Madeline Wiseman. She is a cohost of the New Books in Poetry podcast and is a member of the Science Fiction and Fantasy Poetry Association and the Horror Writers Association. Find her online at www.andreablythe.com.

twitter.com/andreablythe
instagram.com/andreablythe

ABOUT THE COVER ARTIST

Yana Germann is a Russian artist and sculptor based in Saint Petersburg. She developed her artistic skills in the New York Academy of Art, USA and The Repin Academy of Fine Arts, Russia.

All her art is a study of the essence of man in form and eternal issues, about internal transformation. Constant artistic search and balancing on the edges, a game of meanings that reflects duality.

The "LINES" series were presented at numerous international venues and exhibitions; it is part of the private collections of large collectors, including the Agnelli family, Council of Europe as well as the collection of the Presidential Administration of the Russian Federation.

Yana German works with galleries worldwide and is a member of numerous exhibitions. Paintings and sculptures by Yana German are in private collections in Russia, USA, Sweden, Italy, France, Switzerland, Austria, England, Argentina, UAE.

Website: www.yanagermann.com

 instagram.com/yana.germann

INTERSTELLAR FLIGHT PRESS

Interstellar Flight Press is an indie speculative publishing house. We feature innovative works from the best new writers in science fiction and fantasy. In the words of Ursula K. Le Guin, we need "writers who can see alternatives to how we live now, can see through our fear-stricken society and its obsessive technologies to other ways of being, and even imagine real grounds for hope."

Find us online at www.interstellarflightpress.com.

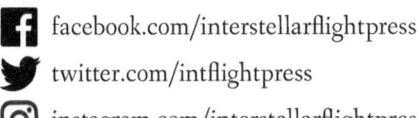

facebook.com/interstellarflightpress
twitter.com/intflightpress
instagram.com/interstellarflightpress

RECENT RELEASES FROM INTERSTELLAR FLIGHT PRESS

The Manticore's Vow by Cassandra Rose Clarke

The Manticore's Vow collects three stories set in the world of *Magic of Blood and Sea*, all exploring the origins of some of its most memorable characters: Naji, the scarred assassin, Marjani, the pirate queen, and Ongraygeeomryn, the man-eating manticore. Explore a world of dangerous magic and thrilling adventures with this trio of gorgeous, swashbuckling tales.

Local Star by Aimee Ogden (Forthcoming 2020)

Triz is a greasemark guttergirl whose world just got a little more complicated. When her ex Kalo comes back from a battle with the Cyberbionautic Alliance, Triz wants nothing more to ignore him. As a woman who's been on her own her whole life, she's not sure if she wants to be a part of a new quadfamily. That is until she's forced to join up with Kalo to save her lover Casne and her home hab. A polyamorous space opera with a fast-paced, action-packed adventure that's sure to punch you in the feels.

www.ingramcontent.com/pod-product-compliance
Lightning Source LLC
Chambersburg PA
CBHW060506080526
44584CB00015B/1576